بِسْمِ اللهِ الرَّحْمَنِ الرَّحِيمِ

When My Absence Becomes a Moon

New & Selected Poems

by
Laureta Rexha

Crescent Books

Crescent Books

Prepared and Typeset
by Erzen Pashaj

Paperback
ISBN: 978-1-954935-09-9
Subjects:
Poems | Faith | Rumi
Kosovo | Islam

First edition
Text proofread by Avni Spahiu
Copy edited by Stella Williams
Cover image: IntergalacticDesignStudio,
istockphoto.com.
Cover design by Stella Williams and
Elipse Productions.

Printed in the United States of America

Praise for Laureta Rexha's
When My Absence Becomes a Moon

"Within wonderfully visual tensions—winter and spring, perception and truth, stagnation and rebirth, waxing and waning—Rexha reminds us to find the peace that is all around us: in a waterfall, a painting, a city, prayer. Stunningly delicate and impactful!"

—Crescent Reviews

"Laureta Rexha's poems are a journey through a landscape of self-discovery, confession, and eventual contentment. Each poem captures a milestone in this journey."

—Wael Almahdi, author of *A Breeze from the East*

"Laureta Rexha establishes herself as a poet who explores and offers her own responses to the drama of modern humanity, from their relationship with the Creator to the individual's relationship with themselves amidst their crisis of alienation. Regarding the information conveyed in her verses, it can be said that it is measured and, for the most part, not explicit, requiring effort to decipher. This is certainly connected to the author's worldview, which is guided by morality and a belief in the recipient's ability to absorb subtle information."

—Milazim Krasniqi, author of *Rigjetja e Vetes*

"Both a profound observation on the facets of conversion and a love letter to God's creation, Laureta Rexha's *When My Absence Becomes a Moon* guides the reader through a rediscovery of humanity and the universe ... While inner peace can be found, the path remains challenging, with the world continuing to present its pains and uncertainties. Laureta's work captures both the innocence of conversion and the inevitable coming of age that all of humanity experiences ... Your mind will have traversed many planes of thought and wonder by the time the book is done, and you'll yearn to take that trip again.

—**Warren Clementson**, poet and primary school teacher

"Rexha's collection of poems gives us pause for patient reflection, laden with urgency, of a universe locked within the human soul. Navigating between distant galaxies, the change of the seasons, to the beating of one's heart and ticking of the clock deep in the night. To the laughter of children, and the familiar sights of her beloved city streets, to the quiet restraints of her familiar home that she longs to leave but always returns, where it forever shapes her soul. Like the girl who does not know how to leave, Rexha leaves us loving, accepting, but wanting more. Reminding us of the profound transitory nature of life, like the scent of a white flower we have missed in our haste and the realization of the moment gone and the splendor transformed. A beautiful dance between the mundane and sublime."

—**Brandon Mayfield**, author of *Grains of Destiny*

"Rexha's collection of poems is a breathtaking journey through Divine love and the beauty of life. Her vivid imagery and emotionally resonant language struck a deep chord with me as a fellow poet. What sets Rexha's work apart is her unique ability to weave these themes with such grace and clarity, creating a tapestry of words that feels both timeless and refreshingly original. Her poetry offers a perspective that is deeply personal yet universally relatable, making this collection a truly remarkable and unforgettable experience."

—**Flamur Vehapi**, author of *Verses of the Heart* and *A Cup with Rumi*

Dedication

I dedicate this book to my beloved parents, who instilled in me the love for learning and knowledge. I thank them for presenting to me a small, modest library when I was a child, which was to become my greatest inspiration in the long years of my future education and my writing career.

Also by Laureta Rexha (in Albanian)

Verë me diell të djegur, 2024

Më përcjell nga larg lutje besimtarësh, 2022

Nën qiellin e parë, 2020

Contents

Preface

It took me years to bring this collection of poetry into English. Written in the aftermath of my undergraduate studies and continuing through my Master's program and beyond, these poems mark the beginning of my writing journey. They capture the discovery of my life's purpose as I first embraced Islam and the determination that drove me to pursue a multifaceted journey of spiritual, professional, and personal growth.

These poems are deeply significant to me for many reasons, containing the essence of who I am. They reflect the peak moments of spiritual fulfillment, the tensions and struggles of maintaining my faith, and my quest for self-realization—a quest that has been central to my scholarly pursuits. Through these verses, I have found solace, hope, and strength in my darkest moments. They have also allowed me to discover the beauty of life and transcend the constraints of fear, stepping into a world of contemplation, meaning, and sensibility.

Looking back, these poems feel like a testament to my life's experiences, evidence of my existence, and a record of my gradual maturation. They reflect my search for the deeper truths of both the visible and invisible worlds that surround me. In these poems, which are a reflection of my faith in God, I have always strived to write with honesty and a courageous literary freedom. Truth is one of the major moral values of Islam, and literary freedom is the vast field where I let my verses roam, giving them space to be born, to grow, and to find their place in my work. Freedom is my most fundamental human value, and I could never be a poet—or truly Muslim—without it. In these poems, you will find that everything I speak of is part of this free spiritual and literary universe—a universe I have wandered in since childhood, where I am both nothing and everything at once. It is from this nothingness that I find my absolute and my true self. These poems give me the courage to reveal my deepest sensitivities and grievances, without fear that they will go unheard.

These selected poems, drawn from three of my Albanian poetry books, represent different stages of my poetic development. As I delve deeper into poetic verse, I also delve deeper into the exploration of the self. I believe that poetic thought serves as a tool for portraying my inner journey through the simple and complex endeavors of daily life.

The Author

Introduction

Within each of us exists a silent voice that calls us to listen, a voice that strives to reveal the deepest secrets of our soul, a voice that, if heard, can teach us the language of the heavens. The great mystical poet, Rumi, heard this voice in such a state of inspiration and wrote, "Listen to the silence. It has so much to say."

This state of inspiration that opens the universe within us—something one can experience only in the most pinnacle moments of life—is the same state in which such poets live all the time. This is why every word of poets like Rumi shines with a celestial purity—poetry as a reflection of the universe locked within the human soul.

Such is also the poetry of Laureta Rexha. The poems in this collection are imbued with such celestial perfection, with poetry as an instrument of the heavens, like a harp with which the poet Rexha plays her beautiful song dedicated to love, in the highest sense of the word.

Rexha's personal experience, her faith, and her love for the Absolute, are presented in the light of universal love through the simple and ordinary life of a young girl, a life filled with love for the things that surround her, such as the elements of nature, her dearest people, and through her daily preoccupations and life's uncertainties. Through these fragments that compose her life, Rexha shows that, nevertheless, one has much more to seek in life, a necessary journey to undertake, a path that leads towards a higher love. Rexha brings every word to life, and anyone who reads her poems can see the bare words of the soul, clothed in their living form, in search of this love.

In Rexha's poetry, we hear the pure voice of love—the intimate whispers of the beloved in search of Love, feeling the happy heart melting for this love, which she has managed to distinguish and recognize in a different form and manner.

Rexha's poetry is filled with metaphors, mainly those related to elements of nature. Within this symbolic language, the "darkness" she walks through at the beginning of her journey, for example, in the poem "I Step Into the Last Stair" but also in "Night Prayer," is essentially a darkness that is necessary to illuminate oneself. According to the language of metaphysics, only one who manages to recognize the darkness within themselves can find the true light. Secondly, "darkness" also refers to the unreality of the earthly world or life, which is nothing but an illusion according to the language of Sufism. In this sense, "darkness" functions as a veil that obstructs human vision, but through love and devotion, one can approach the light of the Absolute.

Even in another poem, "Home," the symbolic language is omnipresent. Here, the home does not refer to the family hearth but to the home of being, because by feeling the presence of true love—through the synchronization of the human being with elements of nature (the river, the lush nature)—the poet understands that the safest hearth and true paradise is what she has built within herself and not the external reality.

In her poetic verse, winter represents the soul separated from God; the waterfall is the perfect beauty of God; the wind is God's life-giving breath; when we hear about the sun, it symbolizes the inner awakening of the spirit, thus, the power that awakens the truth within us; the rain is God's grace; the flowers are the garden of Paradise. Rexha's poetry blooms with love for God. Every life experience she has is a consequence of this divine love that serves as a rebirth for her soul.

Art beckons us only as much as it reveals about our most hidden selves. In this sense, it can be said that art and the observer are one. And precisely, the poem "Painting of My Heart"—which remains one of my favorites from this collection—speaks of this relationship: the observer, mesmerized by the painting she has placed on her room's wall, in a moment of epiphany, discovers that the figures, contours, and the light cast in the painting (which seems to change form constantly), are, in reality, just a reflection of the observer's heart. The work of art as a reflection of the human soul, within which images and figures live just as beautifully. And another metaphor: Rexha's vision to see God everywhere, thus, seeing every part of the creation of the universe as a reflection of divine greatness. Every detail of this world is God's work so that man can know the Truth and learn the secrets of Love.

Rexha's poetry attempts to show us this truth and, likewise, how to open the treasure in which the most precious secrets of love are found. Through her words, we enter the hidden room of the heart, hear its intimate whispers, and see the endless story of love between the human soul and God.

Just like looking before a mirror, Rexha's poetry serves as a mirror in which everyone can see deep into their heart, and moreover, understand the infinite greatness of what we can become.

Dr. Sazan Kryeziu
Assistant Professor of English Literature,
Fehmi Agani University in Gjakova, Kosovo

THE GIRL WHO DOES NOT KNOW HOW TO LEAVE

I would like to keep a grudge just for once
for all the beautiful days that don't repeat,
but I am still the girl who forgives
and swallows old poisonous grief.
I would like to go so far
that my absence becomes a moon.
I would like just for once to keep a grudge
but alas, I am this girl,
who does not know how to leave!

WATERFALL

Waterfall of life
stands upon our sky
like a meteor
runs across the worlds
we have built forever.

Words fall,
tears drop
and we can't even blink

These words I am putting here with the ink
are everything that ever fell for our sake.

SUMMER WITH A BURNT SUN

I will come back anyway
Like an unmistakable season
Through the long roads
During slow summer months
When the heat itself becomes anesthesia
Of my own distraction.

I still don't know
What is wrong with everything
And this summer heat
I just want a heavy rain to fall
Or a mad wind to blow
And to take me for days
In its senseless fury ...

I will come back anyway
Through the fresh evenings
Of another summer
With a burnt sun
And a new moon.

Maybe when the time will have passed
When even the season itself is changed
You will suddenly understand
That I was not afraid of love
But of not being with you.

THE WHITE FLOWERS' SCENT

Across the green valley filled with white flowers
along the pathway where a distant summer I passed by
with haste
that autumn day, I slowed down my walking
and took a look at the place where the flowers did not exist.
A gray sky that day was standing above me
those flowers were vanished by a long summer heat
that sun was hidden by the clouds of a lonely fall
so I reflected on the path where I had stopped purposefully
and I wondered if the passage through life's seasons
had made me wiser at all!

A FOREVER I WANT TO KEEP

My city sleeps in my consciousness
I walk its temporary streets with a forever in me
I look after some broken dreams in my sleeves.
Let me pretend I leave it altogether,
the sleeves, the steps, the city.
I can try to mend the houses, the roads, the places,
everything has to change
but the heart, the people, the feelings,
for these, there is no oblivion left.
I search everywhere for new things,
but my heart rejoices so much in what has been
it wants to keep even the hurt, the grief, and the aches
in a forever wrapped tight,
my heart wants to keep everything.

MY SAJDAH

You have been my best companion for so long,
the bridge to draw me closer to my Lord.
You have taken all my needs
and sat them down in your lap
as if they were yours
when they were mine.
You have taught me to come back
in every struggle
and every joy,
that's why:
I know no other way to endure
this fragile life
with my human heart but with you.
My dear sajdah,
my best companion,
I thank God for every prostration
when I submit myself to Him through you.

THE FORGETFULNESS
OF A PALESTINIAN GIRL

I think I knew it from the beginning
why that strange man
from the distance
said I looked like a Palestinian girl
that Tuesday morning
when I, overflown by the curtain of oblivion
could not even grasp
a war in Palestine.

But from that day on
for months I saw from the screen
how a believer there
every day prays his *Salat al-Khauf* [1]
and a girl without having much time
to think about small matters
there comes a time
when she forgets even her beauty
so when she finally accepts her destined end
and smells the scent of Paradise,
only then, *ya Rab*, [2]
I understand why she forgets everything ...

---

[1] The "prayer of fear."
[2] Lit. "O Lord."

JUNGIAN[3]

I want to awaken from this deep grief
Without pain
Without loss
But I once heard it is not possible to do so
Even if you wake up from a dream
You will lose some illusion
Which kept you deceived on the other side
Buried in some kind of relief

As for the one who filled a greater space in my life
And suddenly isn't there the same
Grieving for him is deep.
I come to a new consciousness therefore
Almost every single day
I climb all the difficult stairs of pain
I awake endlessly from a long night's sleep.

---

[3] In this poem I understated Carl Jung's concept about the awakening of the consciousness through the experience of pain.

THE BURNING OF THE SUN

There is a heat outside
a strange loneliness
in the trees that wave freely
in forty-degree temperature.
Everything is tied well
with the threads of predestination
although inside every possible world of mine
a parting is burning
that makes the earth and the sky fall apart
perhaps this is my Apocalypse!

There is a heat outside
and I five times embrace the earth
five times a day I drink from the promised rivers
I search to connect with the sky
to meet myself far gone in oblivion.

There is a heat outside
during the day the earth in prayer learns how to breath
for the last time there's nothing left to do
to save my Universe even the sun burns in grief!

GENTLE TOUCH

I lay my head on the ground
and listen hard to the song of this life
a whole universe sinking in my soul
a vision of an opening dwelling in my eyes

A gentle touch all over my skin
a wind permeating secretly in me
there are stars I have never asked to admire
and a few skies above
I have never seen.

SHORT STORY

In our little home, every day is the same
when I finish everything, I start over
but I am happy—I have my own God
and another world of mine,
every now and then I build castles
of good thoughts
and they shine beyond it.

In our little home
every day has something to tell me.
My mother thinks I should never leave
and it hurts to tell her that one day I will.

Whoever knows the pathway to peoples' hearts
knows what I am talking about,
knows everything.

NIGHT PRAYER

She was praying in the night all alone,
a prayer never done before,
the prayer of night was called
she was kneeling
she was standing,
all the world seemed distanced.

It was time to stand alone,
time to talk to the One.

Somewhere in the middle of the room
the heart of darkness dissolved,
God will show her the way.

BLUE MIDNIGHT

It is midnight already
everywhere in my room
and in the spaces where the eyes cannot see
there is a voice that murmurs.
I think how November left home
a few days ago
like an abandoned child
As carelessly as it could.

Ask me about November now
As you do for absences
As you do for everything of this fall
For in my bed there is a pain that murmurs
it sleeps once a week
it enters everything I do
it eats with me,
takes ablution sometimes
and asks me, and asks me
she says:
I want you to heal my every wound!
It is midnight and the air is somehow colored in blue
I opened the window just to let its breath in
I think I will pray to The Forgiver for forgiveness solely
and I will pray for so long
until the shackles around
and the veil of sin across the room of the heart
softly break!

THE PERFECT HOSTESS[4]

I think I will shut down the monitor and this view with
a hand
entering the Mirage of the night with downcast eyes
I keep thinking of the woman I read about
named after the Perfect Hostess
and the grand demand of this modern life.
All I want is to let her free
from these parties that don't entertain
this feeling of her being so vast in a room
losing her vision through the windowpane.
Tonight I think I will shut the book I can't read
I will make the prayer of turning with bare hands
empty of me,
empty of all.
All I care is how my curtain will drop
the true victory is finding myself
and for one party of mine that I leave behind
I ask God to forgive me for all the dancing ...

---

[4] A reference to a character in Virginia Woolf's *Mrs. Dalloway.*

I STEP INTO THE LAST STAIR

I step into the last stair
Of this dark
profound height.

I crawl once more
until I reach the door
where all my questions arise.

I stop.
Never thinking that I have to know
all the answers.

I rise again in this journey,
and it matters.

HOURS

Do not ask me how I became this way
I feel more than the rest
how life slips through the hours.

For example today I crossed the seven skies
and sat wide in the universe.
It takes years for the body to reach it
it took me years to write my poetry there
my words with branches toward the sky
roots in the ground,
planted through the streets and rivers,
blooming at crossroads,
at the stations of waiting.

Do not ask me much and listen
I know the call of the rise of the day
and the farewell of the dawn,
separation of people.
And those strange fireworks of longing
that I witness,
soon melting in simple puzzles.

Life is a moment of flickering,
a passing journey,
a collage of wishes and manifold rainbows
meanings coming out of little things
wide spaces filled with light in front of my eyes,
and my soul mounting the last home of mine,
marching through the skies, eternally!

WHY DON'T YOU COME

You came to me in autumn's first breathing,
I wondered why it took so long.
To see the world in your eyes,
out of my own.

You came to me all at once,
and then every other day quite so often ...

Now I still wonder how you left so far.
Why don't you come to me?
Why must all the doors be closed?!

NEVER-ENDING LIGHT

I saw there were stars in you
and thought they were mine.

I jumped from a distant galaxy
dreaming of being caught.

One by one I counted them
and wished to behold
their gleam,
their never-ending light
for which I left the world.

I WILL ASK ABOUT YOU

It is difficult to ask you about anything
even if you respond,
but I will continue.

I will ask about you in every prayer.

NAMELESS

I refuse to name it but I call it fate
this thing I have made myself
out of loneliness and pressure
that keeps telling me what is wrong.
From these feelings, I have obliged myself
the weight of holding what I seemingly can't.
There is a bridge I have tried to build out of nowhere
in this outer fragile world
now knowing what I really fear.
My entire self and my feet tremble
every time I want to walk through it.
This thing in front of me
isn't the next forty-year distant tree of a life I intend to live
but I, torn in this temporary middle
depart in every shade.
And only you,
sun in this changing sky,
only you remain.

HOW WILL THE SKY SPEAK THIS WINTER

Something falls with the first snowflakes
a new cemetery is washed in white,
I wonder: how will the sky speak this winter ...

SOMEONE ELSE'S HOME

You go into someone else's home
The table filled with sweet things
the sound of a half-closed door
and there you step

You happen to be a girl
you happen to be a man
the same welcome,
the same test

You walk into someone else's home
the road leads you back,
you forgot yourself,
you forgot the universe
for just a little bit!

THE DISTANCE

I don't understand why I am so distant
and I have searched the nearness
in the longest night,
in the last prayer
in solitude with God.
I have not asked for this minuteness
that knocks at the last hour ...
I don't know why I am so distant from this Greatness
this heavy solitude that gathers nights with grace ...

... maybe only to awaken from a dream.

THE END OF THE YEAR

By the end of this year
the old song sets forth
ranging through the corners of this room
and upon the roof
the sound of eruption wants to burst out

From what has been left inside
you can see very little,
but across the streets you can see everything
vitality, running and movement and love

It's like all the moments of life have gathered together
yet for each of us a single sky

From what I can tell,
twelve months I have been roaming in the vast circle
daring to jump from the curiosity to meet its end

By the end of this year everyone is giving their greeting
and debts they had with themselves they pay

For a while everything seems finished
and strange as if meeting with life!

THE GIRL WITH THE RED JACKET

In my old red jacket
which I wore for so long
and never got tired of it
there may have fallen dust.
Or else, maybe there was another girl
who was promised to have it
after me
who now wears it casually
a girl other than me
who lives quite another life.
In the street where I used to walk
There are less sidewalks
absent is my slow meditative walk
and all kinds of walks to university.
In that street that I gaze at so often
from where the people pass by
in pedestrian lines
I often wish to walk.
Maybe I will be that young girl again
the girl with the red jacket
the girl who runs from station to station
who dreams about life
and knows she can win.
I want to meet that other part of me
who I knew so well
That girl isn't afraid of anything!

PRESENCE OF YOU

You walk through this path of life
love grows with you each day
I see it when I look out of this window,
and you're always there

How can I measure your pain and your joy
the hopes you nurture so often
endless are the possibilities to measure your life
a sacrifice you have not chosen

Into the walls of our home I stare
and I hear your voice for years
wanting to be heard through them
or somewhere in life

How many battles you have overcome
how many pharaohs you have conquered

I sometimes look at you
and I am afraid that time is walking by so fast
without having done a righteous step towards you

I have never won over the devils that keep me away from
your lap
and that I should come in submission I know
as a daughter, and a child

Mother, your name is beyond this small world
but you don't mind me going round in standstill
I am still looking for love in places
though I know, it comes free in your hug

Mother, even when you're close
with faults that won't pay, I quarrel
With days that pass so soon I thrust,
why don't they fill enough with the presence of you!

IN ANOTHER WORLD

In the wide lightless space
I forget there are doors
tied in the chains of impossibility
and with my eyes closed I open my book

Several times I turn the same pages
I confront myself
I draw back and get tired
and yet in my prime

In my own self four seasons are changing,
but you see me in another world!

WAITING

Through the narrow corridor
the longest steps are treading ...

Only today on the stairs of waiting time stopped
and the dreams of people came crawling
towards the center of the world.

In the shape of an image
the shapeless is ruling over me
here inside these walls
wherein hope echoes often
I realize that light illuminates the end.

Through the narrow corridor
the longest steps are treading
seeking the way I do,
their own universe!

WITHOUT GOD

Abandoning you is like being thrown into a desert,
always thirsty and needy,
without knowing where that comes from

Finding you is like returning to the safest harbor
forever winning—for coming home.

IN THIS EXISTENCE

I walked at the very core
of this existence in fingertips
and saw nothing but you

You are but a mere dream of mine,
our fate torn in two

The morning steps in, fragrant
still a dream,
in epiphany I step.
No one can discern
how this shape began
of me and you, my love,
longing to emerge
like truth in ONE

Things that have no recognition do end,
this is what we were in this existence.

THE SEA OF REPENTANCE

Maybe you are that sea
But I wonder if the earth that waits
To become one with you
Agrees to be washed entirely in your prayer.
Maybe you are that sea
The sea of a quiet night
When I went out of the fences of a home full of voices
And ran towards the lights
Only to hear your breath.
Maybe everything is small
in front of that breathing
that seeks a long relief.
Maybe even the sea surrenders
towards the guilts that are washed
without making much noise
while the self digs deep till the end of time
looking for itself
until it breaks free from the sand of sins.

RISING

Let the dynasty of this grief fall
let the words fall,
it is time to rise.

VOID

I know I need something
I feel my own self searching for a solution

I wanted to talk a bit,
and I was thinking.
How can I fill the empty glass laying there
when the air itself is leaving,
it wants something bigger to get lost in

You tell me the way of fulfillment, my friend,
through the night I seek myself and peace
can they both meet in that middle

Something restless in me ...
I want it to last longer now
this is the only time I take part in a game
when the world remains silent
and I am not afraid of oblivion

If you say enough, I listen
how I can be astonished,
little do I need to recognize my minuteness

I know I need to become my own queen first,
before I rise,
everything else is possible!

TIMES

Times when I am the least myself
but I go on the same each day,
each day I pay a debt for losing something
and hope the last to lose is my way.

Times when I run out of everything
I sit in the calmness of the room
and point myself first,
who's guilty for not surrendering
to the One who gave you a soul?

Times when the days are longer
because I am missing the key,
and somehow the nights are shorter
because I don't know how to awaken

Times when I see the neighbor next door
how she is fighting for life
and I realize that from the noises
I have not well heard the silences
I have not let my inner voice guide me
and took all the time for granted
I have tried everything, but to see!
That divine vow in *Surah Al Asr* [5]
when I think about it,
that vow should have been enough advice for me!

[5] Surah 103 of the Qur'an.

AS LONG AS YOU EXIST

I dreamt the noblest dream after Fajr
my mother carrying stones
on the other side of the house
you and I sitting at the same table
exchanging smiles.

Can I prolong the moment of bliss
I am still there reading your things
looking at God's generous gift
as if we will be given time.

In waking the dream became ephemeral
it left before I could consume the happiness
of finding you.

But I am okay with the rest of the tale
and the beauty of life there
as long as you exist.

A WORLD IN PASSING

One, two, three steps and more
I walk through this one-way street
listening to my deepest needs,
feeling like I was meant to be here

I stare at the nearby toy store
and look for me as a kid
I stop and find myself in its window
having changed and grown into this girl

I wonder, am I the only one who walks like this
as if I am alone in this street filled with people,
with the cold and the sun together fighting each other
this winter

For days I have been seeing things,
going back and forth through a labyrinth
and just today I feel the freedom to begin

It's the only time that I am true to myself
even if others are watching
with all the movement of life around
there's something that is constantly speaking

Is it the voice of the conscience
or maybe the call of my vision that I've long kept inside
it says that I have been running from what I shouldn't
and held onto everything but God
Something reminds me today in this street and in me,
that this world is passing!

I NEED YOU

Now an embrace would help
maybe the pain will set tonight
along with my regrets

I have punished myself out of mercy
you only see a tear flowing down over my cheeks
my inside screams with the strong desire to both live
and diminish

You have set your arms open
and you are a whole
I am ready to break through
into a place where calmness resides

Maybe I will keep you this way for long
so that I can forget the years spent concealing
and running from the rest

Let me go far this time
as soon as I can reach you
otherwise, I will find no peace.

GUEST PAIN

I have been so afraid to sit with you
being in the dark for so long
the table is carefully set
you come from the farthest land
to have such a welcome!
I have been so afraid of you
that you will come no matter what
I think you were always near
but you appeared after the light.
I have been so afraid to sit with you, o pain
because I see your hunger
and smell your fire
when you come and sit at my own table
you eat and burn everything.
I look at you as if you owe me a life
you unwelcomed guest,
how dare you come when I have nothing to give!

AFRAID TO FIGHT ANOTHER WAR

It came to me through the other voices,
how I am used to hearing these things.
One day all my mornings came like tired soldiers
when I met them, they said: we resigned!
We were afraid to fight another war.

HER

If you see her walking slow like a shadow
you won't see the fire in her soul
the hidden dance of her fears

But stepping closer to her figure
there are strings in her hand and stars in her feet,
you wouldn't think on her face once have fallen tears ...

HOLES

Somewhere between the palms of my hands
And the palms of your hands
There is space yet to be filled
Somewhere between your heart and mine
There is no time left to be.
Somewhere I am learning
To light a candle from scratch
A little further
You are quenching it.
Somewhere there is a big hole
Without you
I am fading inside it.

THE BREAK

Amid the trees, I have stood for years
listening to the forest's thinking

In its calmness, I have dived deep
and been gathered in its branches
to find my place.

High above,
I have wished to listen to the wind
and its love for the leaves as they fall
and the moon's longing to light up the Universe
even in eclipse.

And when the silence had so long surrounded me
in those long nights of escape
in a moment I have wished to rise
so that the forest will never listen
to how much I was broken.

PARTS

How can I tell you everything,
a part of me will always be
somewhere else.

But God, I promise,
I will keep the other here.

IN THIS ROOM

So much time has passed within these walls
the dust that is laying there now needs to be gone.

We gather in another day
it is her, him and her again
the main characters of the story
(the sad comedy of those who are not used to letting go
from the beginning)

The woman mentions plays on human passions
the renaissance of an emotion with a person
I am always between two choices
her answer—that no one is excluded—
makes me lame.

So much time has passed
since these books have been written
and then been put in this room,
just to stand amid them and try to reason
that a life of seeking pays for a single action
and then the time soon comes to leave.

WHY DON'T YOU BRING
ME MY LONELINESS

How come this time does not bring me my loneliness
like that of the mountains
but keeps repeating words in high volume.

Why do you bring me the face of a woman
a mere figure, prone to torture
who does not know my only need.

Why do you keep telling me about companions
that my heart does not yet know.

I think the wind outside has brought her promises
the sky has opened
when I raised my hands to the Only One.

How come this time does not bring me my loneliness
the treasure of wanting and needing nothing.

Tell me,
because I don't find myself in the mirror
when I look for myself!

ON LIVING

From the unexpected
guard yourself tight
wait, but wait for no one
day to day
brick by brick
build yourself like home.

INSIDE POETRY

Inside a poem,
a verge of tears that won't come out
and extinguishing would be its end.
Something is on,
it may be this time words are breaking,
or perhaps I am.
Sometimes I don't know where to look
where to knock
and I just lay waiting there.
They told me words are my weapon
so I began to use them
but they don't know
tasting them is totally different.
The world is shaking
people are fighting,
attacking whatever they can.
The pressure falls like rain
the Divine shows, breathtaking,
from the highest place.
Angels prostrate,
I prostrate,
I know something is happening.
I am coming back round from my ancient prime
to see how long I have stood myself in words,
to see what I have become.

CLEANSING

And
when
the heart
has cleaned
itself
from the dust,
you have the right to look beautiful.

TIME

As you realized your life was slipping
in front of your eyes
you chose to stand still.
You are all those years of yours
you have hidden so much in them,
bravery and strength underneath your sleeves.
You are all of that
and all the days that won't let you go
the same little thing that wants to find shelter
in you just once more.

RED SEAS

A few times I have found myself
like Moses,
in front of the Red Sea,
and wished I had done
what was expected of me.
For the point was not to simply pass
but to realize that God was my only guide!

TRAIN OF LIFE

It is late at night
and the train of life runs harder than ever
upon this clock.
It is two a.m.
I don't know how to light another fire.
I need a reason
if you can relate
this is the only train I have.

DAYS OF QUARANTINE

The days are coming
their spring is hidden beneath their early mornings

The nights are leaving every night
with their moons
half-filled, half-empty

Our homes, and our beds where we sleep
and we do not sleep sometimes

Bright skies calling for forgiveness
every minute

Humanity resisting, struggling
turning towards their God

The days are coming in the cups of coffee and tea,
mixed feelings of foreboding
tomorrow will be fine.

METANOIA

It seems I have never known myself
never have felt truly my being,
reject me my honored wait
fulfill this metanoia of living!

MY PLACE

It is this place that keeps me hostage,
my home,
every street
and every mosque,
the place where I walked long to school
where the winters were long
and the summers short,
seasons full of yearning,
a life projected in dreams.
It is this place that calls me wherever I go
everywhere my heart feels this need,
whenever I leave, I think:
one day I will be coming.

LOVE FOR HIS SAKE

Is it wrong to miss a city,
to yearn for its sunrises that seek answers
and miss its dawns that often answer them.
It so happens, you cannot make your sleep
nor can you go about your day
without thinking that you need something.
Is it wrong to love a city
because of the people who live inside it,
it is not,
I swear, it is not,
when feeling love for Him!

MY GLANCE ESCAPES ME

My glance escapes me,
trees shake once more
their boughs made of smiles and tears altogether,
This time cut off like leaves
upon my solitary shelter

leaves,
their boughs have dreamed fruits already

but I,
I want to stretch my life,
and can't destroy what has come to be,
I can't wish for more,
as I hold on.

Those leaves have dreamed
warm days to see,
this time cut off like leaves,
I want to stretch my life!

I LEARN HOW TO LIVE

There is beauty in the way things end
and how others begin,
how the past winter suddenly frees us
with its deepest breath.
It is almost spring,
amid the trees
the flowers
and the laughs of children
I learn how to live!

MORE THAN JUST A GIRL

I almost don't need a picture to describe you
I can see how you lay your hands on the desk
around so many people in the classroom
and it's like no one can contain
the worth you feel
and how you bloom ...

The spring had come
and we had time for nothing but poetry,
discussing "The Love Song of J. Alfred Prufrock,"
reminiscing the last April.

I almost don't need to say a word,
a courageous girl does not need that
when she is more than just a girl!

WITHIN A STRANGE WORLD

For months I had relied upon a swinging chair
an utopic world I gazed
my mind blowing from a soft wind,
and being fed for a long time
from the temporary presence of other people
I had forgotten that one day I will have to meet
the absence,
suddenly with the uncertainty of everything.

For a while, I stopped and I promised,
this time I will take a good look at myself,
when alas,
I did not know what to see!
Within a strange world,
I was utterly emptied
out of the swinging chair and my world,
suddenly, I had nothing to give!

YOUR SOUL REACHED BY ME

Each thing falls with its lightning
there was darkness and I could not see
the depth of your soul
in all its blazing beauty
was reached by me!

THE CITY OF US

We were in the prime of life
when we met in a small mosque
a blessed Friday of a rainy summer.

I was amazed by my friends since then
the first thing I saw was their bow-downs to prayer
and their reliance on and love for God.

We became close like spring flowers
blooming beside each other in every triumph.

I never thought those days would pass
without us noticing,
like an afternoon.

Then one day, when everything was over,
even our favorite coffees,
our blessed friendship withstood it all.

We had not much
but we had our city that kept us together
and souls filled with awe.

I remember us like the streets of our city
and it feels we have become it.

How come we forgot that life was passing
in that happiness,
when I look back,
it has been years!

SHORES

I have tried to catch the heart
that wanted to jump itself into the vast ocean
the waters were calm
the sun shined in a clear blue sky,
I had nothing to fear.
I let it free, this time.
Let it fall with the simplicity of another
with beauty
with smiles,
I wanted nothing more.
In the room of my home with another view
with the perseverance of a mother
for hours I projected the ending of something.
And though I kept diminishing myself
I silently hoped,
maybe I will fall
I will fall with time.

Frequency had fled away,
departed from the homeland of pain
I did not know what to plant in the new land.
With my head in front
and my heart behind
I felt how I was being removed from
everything.

On the verge of meetings
I had lost my way.
Only today, I see a waterfall
pouring through my shores
with the fall of rain,
I have become a depth
there is no one to help
no sailor comes so far this time
nor you,
nor me!

LORD OF RAIN

Before the rain fell I was utterly folded
and crawled repeatedly in my small sense of self.
When the lightning struck
my roots expanded,
my petals moved,
this is how I learned
I was a slave of the Lord of rain.

YOU ARE STILL FORTY

You are still forty, o Messenger,
tell me how the revelation came
how you woke up from a temporary sleep
for you were the heart of this *Ummah*
and you were the first to be shaken for the sake of
the truth.

You are still forty,
decades of revelation changed through you
the pillar of morals stands still from the example you gave.

It is Ramadan,
you are still forty,
the greatness of Allah still trembles you,
your feet hurt from praying too long
and your eyes have never dried from tears.

It is the blessed month
the wisdom of the Qur'an
teaches us to repent in every verse
your chest opens up towards it every year
then you ascend in the night journey.

You are still forty, o Messenger,
tell me how to stop this waste of time
for I don't know what to say to 1400 years of your absence
when they tell me about you

You are still forty,
but our time is not running the same,
what am I going to tell God when I meet Him
if I have not followed you!

THE WAIT OF THE TRUTH

I was hoping to see you
wearing the light of truth like jewelry
the wrist watch to be on time
and the shoes of never-ending steps
we made towards each other.
But it did not happen
so you can wear whatever you want now
as long as you are here
you may not be too late.
I myself will keep the long dress of faithfulness
and I will keep it for long,
because it looks good on me!

THE STARE OF THE FEELING

The roots of this feeling are deep
its color is solely hope
her scent is all reward
its place is in the soul.
The face of this feeling changes
every day she comes in my embrace
in another form.
The purpose of this feeling is high
why do I stand so low
maybe this feeling will take me
higher than I have imagined.
The beginning of this feeling is a shiver
its morning is full of concern
its noon is acceptance
her night, all submission.
In the life of this feeling
it is me that I seek,
will any of us free the way for the other
because when we both break
with a look, I see everything!

PASSENGER

The long one-way street
From a city to another
With several stopping points
Demands that I get off at every Terminal.
From place to place
Nothing belongs to me
In this journey
Only the good deed remains
As my best companion
And my eyes looking ahead
And my heart seeking restlessly
For the final home
At the eternal station
To where I travel
Towards the Great End.

HER NAME IS NOT PAIN

The other is the thing I carry on with me for years
and tears run down my cheeks ...
inside me, rivers flow unstoppably
until the tide takes on everything.
The other thing I carry on with me is older now
a woman of every shape
small size,
big size,
her body endures every injury
until all the waters of her life run dry.
The other is a pain ingrained in me
it has a voice
it has ears
I simply take a look at it sometimes,
and it screams.
The other is inside and outside of me
I once recorded every sound
I once wrote every word
but in the end, I erased, I erased everything ...

When I look outside of this vast universe
my heart wants to forget
my mind wants to redeem.

When I open my eyes,
and wake up as if from centuries asleep
my eyes look for another space
different from the red room of a Jane Eyre
a colorful universe, to paint from the beginning
a home I can find shelter in and live in it forever ...
The other thing I carry on with me
has breathed enough years
has lived so many seasons
the thing I carry on with me is not my pain!

MY PARENTS' FACES

I try to understand and I know where that grief comes
from
when I look at the face of my dad when he comes back
from work
when I sense my mother's worry when she cooks twice
a day
and the weight of her life never takes advantage of her.
I try to gather that strength only for a few minutes
and all that dedication
when she says: it's been like one hundred years ...!
So I pray to God, I never become the source of their pain
because when I look at my parents' faces,
I am silent, again!

SAVING MYSELF

This self of mine
is the most sacred thing I have
in it I have stored my faith
and my deepest weights.
This self is my first companion
in this life, and the next,
but I did not know it always
so I have lost it frequently.
One day I took a risk
and went so far.
When I realized it
I got back right away.
My self had crashed in the strongest of lands
it took strength to lift it up on her feet
so I sought for it beyond the heavens.
When my hands stood long enough in prayer
and I got rid of the unnecessary,
the door broke open.
(Now listen well,
my self was saved as for it I gave up everything else!)

YOUR NAME SADNESS

I don't know why the silence I run from so often
makes complete sense to me
I took this pain an umbrella for protection
to shelter me on the verge of rain.
I don't know if our names ever met in the constellations
but some skies broke asunder
and I broke with them
when I heard your name sadness in a foreign tongue.

CRESCENT MOON

Some nights I would take
Him as my only Witness
Because I had not even myself left
To feel entirely what I was feeling.
Some nights, just like the moon
I was running in phases
Crescent and lonely throughout a vast sky
While the sound of a clock on the wall
With my heart's sound in my chest
Were the only things making noise in the world.

GIRLS LOVED BY GOD

These girls coming out of school
Little girls
Girls in the first grade,
second grade, third grade
What do they want from me
When they secretly gaze
At any ring on my hands
Or the scarf on my head
That says I am a Muslim.
Pure are their hearts and their gazes
Every time we get on the same bus
And they can't wait to say Salam to me.
To whom belongs that gaze that hesitates not
To greet and shake hands with me
Whenever they get off at the next bus stop.
These little girls in the first grade,
second grade, third grade and more
Seem to be bigger than me
These girls when they greet me first
I am sure God loves them deeply.

THE WOMAN WITH THE DREAM OF A HOME

That woman had black long, combed hair
and only a few strands lay on her shoulders.
She was a simple woman
she raised the little family
and the little home,
the tree that grew in her garden.
She was a woman you only meet once in your life.
For example, as you involuntarily leave home
and fate sends you somewhere far away.
Years went by and I never saw her
never tasted a generosity like hers,
greater than anything she had to give.
Now that she stands in front of me
I see her with the eyes of a little girl.
But I don't know ...
Is she the woman wearing a long dress full of yellow flowers
with strong hands, tired from labor
with the dream of a home, home, home

I still look at her
and I am amazed from the passing years
what have they done to her
and what have they done to me!

This woman has another face now
but I eagerly look for the same heart in her
the same innocent smile I once reached.

She reminds me of a time and me
the family, the union
the comings and the leavings
she reminds me of hunger, hopes, and fallings.
This woman has gone on a long journey in my life
her role is transient
but she still accompanies me on a long road in her village
where I am catching fireflies.
She keeps doing so until I reach home.

COME WIND

Come wind of reunion
teach me the wisdom of this silence
the fruits of this change.
I have become like a stone
that doesn't like to be blown at anymore
and just lay down in my place.
Come wind of fulfillment
and guide me home
I have become numb in this existence,
come wind, give breath to my soul!

I AM MAD AT YOUR LONELINESS

It has a name and it is here
whatever is burning the fires inside me.
If you ask me what's wrong,
I am mad at your loneliness
your loneliness that keeps you away from me.

WHAT I AM WAITING FOR

Let the winds touch me tonight
let the storms hit me
and in their fury, forget everything
let me crawl into the meaning of simple things
let me revive after I have been tired of life
and let it happen what I feel
for often it seems it is just a step further
what I am looking forward to let finally come.

In the very bottom of a filled glass, I will rest
and ask God to save me from what is haunting
and fighting me since forever.

(Because trust me, I know the story of someone
who, in fighting, never manages to win!)

HAUNTED

My words—They haunt me.
One minute I am quiet
and I forget that life is passing me by.
One more day is gone,
and I haven't written a word!
You can't just sit there
and forget that we exist in you, they say.
That you breathe in our flashes of light,
when finding strikes.
I know that, I respond. I know.
How can I forget about you without forgetting
about myself?!

A NEW WAY OF BEING GONE

I wanted to give birth to a new way of being gone.
Something you could never imagine, but feel.
That was it; to feel me being gone.
To feel me coming back, right into myself.
But you never saw it.
I was never really gone when you were there.
When you were there ...

IT IS GOOD TO LOVE

You look at me silently,
for you've known me a lifetime.
You cannot judge me,
nor say to me that the path I have chosen to follow
has a dead end and that it leaves not much to hope for.
All the same, I go on ...
with this courage that does not know any obstacles
listening to your words so calm and full of grace:
that there is nothing wrong in all this.
That it is good to love.

PAINTING OF MY HEART

I bought a painting and put it on the wall
the wall of my room that is always so small
still keeps things bigger than it
I still try to nourish it with my feminine dreams

I looked at the painting almost amazed
trying to find the meaning I miss
I seek something, and need something
yet something bemuses me

I took a step towards the painting
perhaps being closer will be better,
and seeing it with truthful eyes
and seeing it for a second time
makes me think how small I am
towards the thought of someone else
who painted it in a time of bliss
or in a time of need,
who can tell?!

I opened my heart to this evening call
the painting is still there standing on the wall
I saw it was as deep as the sea
some lines there and some rays here
all emerging towards some end
and perhaps this is who I am

For what I see is not a work of art
but rather a simple painting of my heart!

LOVE IS SOMETHING ELSE

You have spent your life running out of doors
always chasing things
and never meeting ends.
You have gone so far that there is no way back
don't you realize that love is something else?!

BECOMING

She is home now.
The miracle was not to see one come
it was she, becoming!

ETERNITY

In that mystic call
When the hands are raised
When cost what it may
The heart surrenders
The Universe takes another form
The earth where you stand
Becomes a cradle
That moves you softly
In the lullabies that are sung eternally
In supplications made only for Him
Who taught you to feel the need
For no one else.
In that mystic call
When the skies are opened
And forgiveness descends softly
Down your cheeks
Without making much noise
You realize that you are not alone.

HOME

I write down my words
they flow like river chasms
I hold dreams of flying
passing through green sceneries

This feeling has no bonds ...
Whatever the future brings on its shore
I shall never feel anymore
the fear of leaving this home I have built from within,
with a river and the scenery green.

Acknowledgements

My deepest thanks for the publication of *When My Absence Becomes a Moon* belong to Allah, the Almighty.

I also thank the amazing people who supported me morally and professionally for the publication. In particular, I thank the Crescent Books team for undertaking this beneficial task so willingly and professionally. I also greatly thank those professionals who edited and proofread my poems through the publication stage: Mr. Avni Spahiu and Stella Williams. I also immensely thank Dr. Sazan Kryeziu for the wonderful introduction that he wrote in regards to the entire poetry collection, esteeming it greatly in literary terms. I am so grateful to him for being a wonderful guide and motivator for me to continue writing in the spirit of heavenly inspiration since the end of my Bachelor's studies.

I finally thank my family, friends and all professors who have read my poetry through the years, and have encouraged me to pursue and develop my poetic verse continually.

About the Author

Laureta Rexha was born in Gjakova, Kosovo. She completed her Bachelor's and Master's in English Language and Literature at the University of Prishtina in Kosovo. She is a poet, researcher, and currently works as a translator at the Fehmi Agani University in Gjakova, her hometown. She has also been involved in research for national and international conferences in topics that intrigue her interest in literature. Since 2016, Laureta has been publishing her poems in several online sources and national anthologies. She is a published author of three books of poetry in Albanian. This is her fourth book of poems, and the first in English.

About Crescent Books

Crescent Books is committed to publishing works that challenge the conventional and celebrate the diverse voices that enrich our understanding of faith, culture, and history. As a small, passionate team of book lovers, we guide authors through the publishing process with editorial freedom and genuine partnership. We are dedicated to producing books that inspire, provoke thought, and entertain, creating transformative reading experiences that connect with a broad audience and open doors to new perspectives on our ever-evolving world.

Other Titles by Crescent Books

A Breeze from the East by Wael Almahdi, 2024

Grains of Destiny by Brandon Mayfield, 2024

Berke Khan of the Golden Horde by Flamur Vehapi, 2024

The World According to Sami Frashëri by Flamur Vehapi, 2024

The Spectacular Escape by Burhan Al-Din Fili, 2023

Atheism Versus Belief by Brandon Mayfield, 2023

Kosovo: A Brief Chronology by Flamur Vehapi, 2023

Verses of the Heart: Poems by Flamur Vehapi, 2021

Ertugrul Ghazi: A Very Short Biography by Flamur Vehapi, 2021

For our titles in other languages, check out thecrescentbooks.com.